PS Cottier & Sandra Renew

V8

V8

ISBN 978 1 76109 382 1

Copyright © text PS Cottier & Sandra Renew 2022

Cover image from getdrawings.com

First published 2022 by

GINNINDERRA PRESS

PO Box 3461 Port Adelaide 5015

www.ginninderrapress.com.au

Contents

Cylinder 6: Utes

Cylinder 7: Consequences

Cylinder 8: Further on

Foreword

We have been colleagues as poets for quite a few years, and we noticed that we both write about cars, trucks, utes and other moving vehicles (and sometimes dead ones). And we noticed that when we read these poems at open mics and poetry readings the audience seems to like them.

We found that we write about cars because they fascinate us. But also because through cars and other moving vehicles (and sometimes dead ones) we can conduct social commentary under the radar. Sometimes the poems are tongue-in-cheek, sometimes outrageous, sometimes quite funny.

It was PS Cottier's idea to collect these poems into one place and also her fixation on the V8 as an object of poetry that led to the arrangement of this collection.

We enjoyed writing these pieces, or finding them in our own archives, and we hope readers like reading them.

Cylinder 1

Modelling the past

Nobodies

Bonnie and Clyde were nobodies without their V8 Ford
joyriding
robbing and killing
punctured with over 100 armour-piercing bullets

Thelma and Louise somebodies in the 1966 Thunderbird
convertible
went from naiveté to 'most wanted'
airborne over the lip of the Grand Canyon

Mad Max odyssey in a 1973 Ford Falcon XBGT
modified
last of the V8s
drifting loner-driver in post-apocalyptic Wasteland

Batman and Robin adventuring in the Batmobile
heavily armoured
tactical assault vehicle in pursuit of evil
wing-shaped fins are every knight's wet dream

Clint and Meryl play Robert and Francesca
1960 GMC pick-up
engine idles, waiting, at traffic lights
leaves the bridges as sixty million romantic dreams

Sandra Renew

The animal tells it like it is

At the garage owned by the museum,
they showed us all the Holdens,
that seemingly indispensable vehicle
for Australian roads.
The first Holden. The last.
And there was a model thylacine
smiling at us, as if to say
extinction is a thing, you know,
whether marsupial or car.
Her stripes. Their wheels.

PS Cottier

Anguish

If it wasn't bad enough that kids
detected the shadow of an English accent
in my vowels, before I took a hammer to them,
flattened them into acceptance,
my parents drove an *Anglia*. Now I would die
for such a classic, perhaps in duck-egg blue.
Then it was a further embarrassment –
a car that spelt the dreaded word Pom
with the very curve of its cute roof.

PS Cottier

love note to a silver ghost (Rolls-Royce 40/50 Silver Ghost, 1907)

my eyes are sun-dazzled by silver, dignified reflection belies
the Spirit of Ecstasy rampant on the bonnet, subtle
forest-green leather seats, an engineering marvel finished with
black-gold plating and hammered copper. I'm writing this in
black and white, can't squander words on beauty, can't write
this car in colour.

Sandra Renew

Not the full Fiat

Pushing up, lying back,
I imagine a Fiat 500
clamped to the end of my toes.
500cc, 500 kilos,
give or take.
I am at 450 kilos, so not
the full Fiat,
but it's like birthing a bambina.
Or bambino, for weight
doesn't discriminate.
My knees swell like tyres.

PS Cottier

When did she become so lonely?

she was ten when she learned to drive a Model T Ford,
converted to carry farm tools and hay bales, daggy sheep,
shovels, and wire-cutters, spare rolls of plain and barbed wire,
pieces of harness for various sized saddle horses –
all the grit of blowing sand

she still drives the track following directions her father shouts
into the wind as she moves off, slow-riding the clutch, stop,
start, break open the bales, sling the slabs onto the sheep
track, a hillside of movement as sheep string out along the
hayline.

she knows the sign at the crossroads – Population 23. she's
been to the city, a dual highway of impatience, no one stops
for anyone. she's been away to school, seen a new world. she's
come back.

check the water level in the dam, the intake pipe still under
water, start the pump, open the tank, clear the trough.
cracking clay at the waterline stinks in the drying sun, wet
cloying mud a false barrier along the yellow water edge.
crows keep their distance, keep their eye in. all they need is
patience.

Sandra Renew

Before the Mustang

It was reliable, comfy as ugg boots,
and just about that chic.
Grey, four-cylinder, economical,
totally un-American.
Not a hint of speed or sprawl.
It was even easy to park,
and slid out of view
before anyone noticed it.
If you wanted to be a spy,
or a private eye, this car
would be the one for you.
You could dwell outside a house
for weeks, before anyone
thought that there was something to see,
something resembling a car.
I loved it, my first new car.
I hated it for its bland compliance
with a view of what should be.
It broke down exactly once,
and the police were hugely surprised.
It had a cavernous boot for shopping,
and no one raced it from the lights,
making sport from nothing.
It is gone now, but I'm sure
someone is driving it, somewhere,
that grey slab of suburban metal,
that practical lump of sleep.

PS Cottier

By their wipers ye shall know them

Our old cars had wipers
determined to remove glass
as well as sheets of rain.
They screeched like banshees,
thin banshees raking at the windscreen.
There was no money for replacements.
My new car senses moisture,
gives an elegant swish,
a mere apologetic frou-frou
as refined wipers operate
with the elegance of a butler.
Would ma'am like dry windows?
Yes, Edwin, this rain is awfully damp.
Sometimes I miss the noise,
of my wonky old cars' wipers,
clawing at the rain like parrots —
parrots screaming their hydrophobia.

PS Cottier

Last run of the Dodge

The Dodge 1923 Tourer was a car so old it had running boards and a concertina-style vinyl hood. It was low-slung, black and the sweep of the body made it somehow sinister, a gangster/hoodlum vehicle. My father took out the back seat, and doors, and all the roof fittings, converting it to a ute to carry bales of hay, bags of oats, drums of fuel and 10/80 rabbit poison. He repaired it often with wire, a hammer, tyre patches. And the registration had lapsed long ago, we knew it was only legal off-road in the paddocks.

There were times however, when the 1956 FJ Holden was away, and my mother was home-alone with four primary school age children. She was forced to decide on a stay-at-home day, (read miss-school day) or driving us five miles to town on an unmade road, narrow, potholed, wheel ruts sump tearing and set like concrete or maliciously boggy, depending on the season. The round trip plus round again for the school pick-up, was a considerable expense of luck and energy, and required a degree of certainty that it would all be worthwhile in the end. A lesser woman would have opted for a rare missed-school day but there may have been other compelling adult reasons to have us all away for the day.

One day, in the Dodge, on the way to school, my brother and I riding the running boards, wild in the hot, dry wind and blowing dust, sisters in the stripped out back area, uncomfortable ballast on loose chaff bags, my mother riding the clutch, deftly changing up and down, sliding through stony creek bottoms, fine-tuned judging of the run-up needed to top a particularly steep bank. The engine suddenly hiccupped mid-roar and stopped. My mother stood on the brake. Twisted the hand-brake ratcheted out full length and yelled at us to chock the wheels with stones and branches. This left the Dodge, unregistered, halfway up a steep bank in the middle of the road.

With a note on a page torn from my homework book, my brother and I were sent to walk the remaining two miles into town to the mechanic garage where a tow truck was sometimes parked out the back. And we were then strictly instructed to go on to school with another note explaining our late arrival.

That afternoon my father collected us from school in the FJ Holden. My mother served chops and potatoes and peas for dinner in silence, lips pursed, squinting eyes saying *don't mess with me tonight*. My father tried some unfunny irrelevant jokes before lapsing into a hurt *I'm the victim too* silence. My brother and I had been in the limelight at school with our recounting of the story bearing several retellings during the day and we were obliviously full of it. The two little sisters ate their dinner beneath the radar and slid out of their chairs early with the promise of someone reading them a story later.

The Dodge reappeared after a decent period of repair time had lapsed but was never again pressed into service for the school run.

Sandra Renew

Suburban tanka

his car so old,
from Time before computers
still does his own repairs,
parts pillaged from car graveyards
on vacant blocks

party bus, balloons
back beat bass booming
through sleeping streets,
stops to let partygoers
chunder on the nature strip

Sandra Renew

Weekend Canberra

he drives his Nissan Pulsar like it is a Jeep Cherokee –
revs it on the roundabouts, does donuts in the cul-de-sacs
at midnight on a weeknight…

from a roadside pick-up pile he finds a mattress with an
unobtrusive water mark
where in normal circumstance a large established stain
of uncertain but certainly disreputable heritage shouts sleaze
from the centre…

slips through the Summernats' street parade on Northbourne
gives the finger to the driver with last-minute brakes on
his souped-up flashy chrome and noise…

thumbs up to the wet T-shirt girl steaming, posturing…

on Monday he coaxes a lady bird beetle onto his same
finger-for-fingering
and carries her to a wind-burned leaf in a bottle brush tree
out of the way
of workman's boots and mates spewing last night's fun-time
into the garden mulch

Sandra Renew

Body parts

In the ice cream shop in Tilba Tilba,
discovered by the guy from Narooma auto electrics and body
shop,
is a once-missing body part of a dismembered 1961 EK Holden,
(burgundy duco, cream on top, chrome wheels),
back section violently blowtorched from the body and turned
into a cushioned sunken couch –
authentic restoration depends on finding the widely flung
original sections

Sandra Renew

Cylinder 2

Just Drive

Driving tips from my mother

She always slowed down way before lights,
in case they change to red. I can still see
the desperate efforts of other drivers
swinging around the sudden roadblock.
She inched towards an always possible stop,
causing mayhem through too much safety.
Loud horns accompanied every drive –
she'd call those motorists *rude and reckless.*
They should all lose their licences.

Air conditioning is dangerous, she said.
It makes you too comfortable. As if torrents of
sweat falling into the eyes might not detract
from the hideous possibility of coming
within a hundred metres of a traffic light
and not slowing down to thirty k an hour.

Driving was always something to be dreaded.
The idea that it might be fun, a jaunt,
took me many years to discover,
haunted as I was by an unseen manual
of endless don'ts. *Don't listen to music.*
Don't go to the speed limit, stay below.
What are you smiling about? This is dangerous.

I drove with an exploded airbag,
before they were even invented.
Twenty years, it took me,
give or take, before I learnt a different way,
and pushed the pedal (the one on the right)
to a suddenly gleeful floor. G-forced back
into a delicious curve of seat,
I made the engine sound louder
than childhood's passing horns.

PS Cottier

to the city

smells of dead cow, cracked clay shrinking
dam's edge, stagnant water, dying reeds –
all this was the end of it.

bag packed with clean city clothes,
last week's pay (already half spent)
thin back-pocket wallet –

salt leavens the dust of leaving

the ute sings through the crossroads
turns onto the highway
for the last time

over the sweep of skyline
the city is a headline –
crass cacophony, brassy neon, promising

like she knows where she's going

smell of petrol on hot tar,
takeaway, giveaway *room to rent*
signs smell of lonely

country camouflaged as city
dust and salt more than skin deep
take the turns through the traffic lights

every street is the start of it

Sandra Renew

Away

Grey-green fog. Gnarly wave road breaks through mountain
forest. Punk cycad heads poke through undergrowth, black
boots buried in soil. Glimpse of lyrebird, harptail plucked to
pungent hum of chainsaws. Asthmatic engine chokes on its
own emissions. Wombat balls play unruly games with tyres.
Brown smell of coffee from last stop. Acute accent of seatbelt
splices chest. Hands read ten to two, two when shifting.
Modest wood, trucks flaunt on shameless corners. Carpaccio
of kangaroo, fat ravens eye-delving. We steal glances. Wheel
past wrappers and cans. End of week, work punctuation. Car
coughs up the incline. Wending.

PS Cottier

walking both away and into

an old felt hat
brings back memories
of the desert treks
no footprints for 500 kilometres
Oh! the space of it

silence
wind worrying sand
leaves evidence
of prescience
sand swirls, ridges dry desiccated
ephemeral waterholes

Parchment desert spreads a full vista, wrinkles of dunes,
spinifex and dune grass as far as far. Wildflowers, pink and
yellow, already dried, a gift from the parched. Walking both
away and into. Steps punctuated by camel bells, creaking
camel saddles, occasional sighs from the camel string,
soft-voiced cameleers. Rush of budgies, thousands
fingerprinting the blue – unison magic.

line of horizon
clear and uncluttered along dune tops
on the ridge, camels
minuscule in perspective
underlining the enormity of universe

Sandra Renew

Summernats (and Floriade)

Cars planted in street beds shine brighter than tulips.
Fragrant noises bloom orange in jam-packed ears.
Thick rubber paths curl through stolid roads
as tangled black snakes make love to tarmac.
A Bathurst of sudden young centaurs
frolics through Inner North sleep,
dancing quick Dionysian steps
to horny symphony of beep.
These are the very people who pay
for Canberra's narcissistic reflections.
Just once a year their exhaustive rites
relieve us from dull bulbous perfection.
Their swift intervention smells of summer,
breathes air into comb-over city's bald plan.
Then tents are uprooted,
and the breeze moves on.

PS Cottier

In the Hindu Kush

breathe in
breathe out
old light
light years of travel
to reach us
unfolding remembering
old light
comes from beginnings
as well as endings
breathe in
breathe out
the black SUV follows us into the sky, close up our bumper,
as we climb into the peaks of the Hindu Kush, through the
Salang tunnel down into northern Afghanistan.
in the Hindu Kush,
heading for Sheberghan, past Mazar-e-sharif
our eyes meet in the mirror, both looking back,
Fawad frowning…we look back again
black cars, black windows,
right on our bumper for the last thirty minutes
we are in Dostum's country
three-car convoy pulls out, passes us, horn blaring,
driver's hand flicking at us through the side window…
a warlord…
we're in his way, and he's late.

Sandra Renew

the wrecked cars (haiku)

the wrecked cars
restart themselves
zombie burnouts

PS Cottier

Chancers

Cement like polished stone in the arches above us. Roar of traffic overhead like the recriminations or accusations of angels When we turn off the boom box, the fog causes no echo. Reeds and clear water, frogs sound, embedded in the silence. We watch the car, parked, sitting in shadow on the gravel verge.

After a moment, the driver, formless, anonymous in heavy coat, knitted beanie, heads off up the slope to the highway without looking back.

Easing open the driver's side door. Lean across to open the caddy and the glovebox. Nothing. A jumble of junk, chip packets, old Bic lighter, one glove, random receipts. No cigarettes. No cash stuffed into the back. No blood. We take the blanket from the back seat, dog hair and old car-sick vomit.

Chancers, going nowhere. Too gormless to make a plan says her dad. *Leave them alone* says her mother. *We can wash the blanket.*

Sandra Renew

Hand ballet

The improvisation within well-known moves,
the slowing shift to first, at the lights,
the quick tap to second, the elaborate
leap across and up to transitional third.
The glad movement down, forth to fourth,
when the path clears into open smile.
Manual ballet, performed as you read the road.
The foot plays its part, too, the clutch pressed
into service, to allow the hand its sweet moves.
Perhaps it is a *pas de deux*, the foot and hand
moving as one, until a gear is missed,
and the music grinds into wincing noise.

Automatics are taking over, stodgy yet whiny,
replacing the dance with unseen plod.
But they'll prise my dear gearstick
from my once dancing dead hand.

PS Cottier

Silent combat

As if having treats was usual, travelling
between Ballarat and Geelong on the Midland Highway
we littered the back-seat vinyl of the Holden –
Mintie wrappers, and Jaffas crushed
into the carpet behind the front seat barrier.
They were busy
in silent combat. Flying under the radar,
we gorged ourselves on sugar
careless of our self-control and fragile teeth.

Sandra Renew

A taxi to Sheremetyevo

I reached for my seat belt
and the driver gave a gesture
meaning there's no need.
He drove on packed roads,
wider than I was used to,
weaving in and out of traffic.
I longed for a seat belt,
but didn't want to offend.
He asked where I was from
and I answered.
He thought I said Austria,
(not good as we passed
a memorial marking how
the NAZIs came so near Moscow)
but eventually he understood.
He took both hands off the wheel,
and mimed a kangaroo.
I nodded, enthusiastic,
trying to hide my great longing
for a piece of well-placed fabric.
That was back when the USSR
was the name of the country.
Do they have more need
of fastened seat belts now?

PS Cottier

Siglio

The rusting vehicle on blocks
in the grounds of the church
is a *siglio*: a small, unauthorised marvel,
because the vehicle is an American Jeep,
and the churchyard is deep in Siberia.

The marvel is how the jeep, the icon of the US military
overcame the hostilities
of the Cold War, between the US and the USSR,
and entered Russia, and how it defied
the impossible logistics of ten thousand kilometres
of snowed-in taiga forest with rail-only access,
and sat for years under the gaze of the Old Believers
as they went to and from their church of icons.

The two volumes of poetry, in Russian,
in the second-hand bookshop in Irkutsk,
are a *siglio*: a small, unauthorised marvel,
because the books contain the poems
of Alexander Pushkin,
whose political poetry from exile in Siberia
was censored by the Czar,
and who died for honour in a private duel
in 1837, at the same age as Byron died,
and the marvel is that in 2013 his words
of love and politics still stand for
the juxtaposition of passion and revolution
that travellers to Siberia seek in the cities,
founded by exiles and dissidents,
on the east–west rails.

Sandra Renew

Love travels with us

Love travels with us along the rails in Siberia.
Love is scrawled as graffiti on the wall
of an abandoned village house in Mogocha.
I love you OK! is in carefully blocked letters
on the jetty at Baikal,
in a concentrated summer with dandelions gone to seed.
Alexander is in love with his unattainable princess
in Irkutsk, writing of troikas and roses.
Determined lovers promise their undying commitment
on the city lookout in Vladivostok, and
on the footbridge of a thousand padlocks in Irkutsk,
close the lock on the rail and throw the key to the river and wind.
Street graffiti is underfoot in paint and chalk,
pledging, avowing, declaring love in letters four feet high.
The bride in a wedding party in Novosibirsk
has Marilyn Monroe tattooed on her calf and seven-inch heels.
LOVE is stencilled on the inside of an empty goods wagon
on a siding in Yekaterinburg.
The Ruby Kazan football team has a ruby-red bus
gifted from the city that loves them,
and a heart is ringed in lights against the sky
on the roof of a building in downtown Kazan.
And in the Kremlin Armoury, surrounded by the wealth of Russia,
there are silver horseshoes with heart-shaped cut-outs.
Love is on the rails in Siberia, and it travels with us.

Sandra Renew

Before the satellite

We drove with the Melways
open, leafing through pages,
trying to make the route
horizontal, as the car swept
through endless streets.
Flipping was an art form,
the down and up glance
yesterday's mobile phone,
but legal and habitual.
Every glovebox in Melbourne
sported a Melways, and Sydney
clutched its UBD.
Now there's a woman
trapped in the glovebox,
of variable accent,
beamed down from above.
She tracks our movements,
informs us to stay straight,
or to merge slightly left,
positioning us, freed from
the gentle rustle of paper,
and the desperate flick
at every red light.

PS Cottier

Cylinder 3

Two wheels

Bikes

they take their time entering the new city, ostentatiously
slowing to the speed limit
inked insignia on faded denim, jeans torn, detailing
embroidered with a line from Cohen…like a bird on a wire

scuffed boots, soles worn where they've taken the weight of
stopping and starting from P plate to upgrade, Northbourne
Avenue filleted by the raw, new railway…
now a single line of throbbing CCs, rumbling revs, parades
their menace and my insignificance –

I'm reflected in her helmet visor for a moment when she
slows for the lights, the one hundred bikes crowd in beside
her before sweeping on
I want to be here for the end of it

Sandra Renew

Failure to zoom

I failed to get my bike licence twice,
once in a fenced off area,
with bizarre rituals of steering,
and once because I could not emergency brake
without slowing down first.
And yet, all the time, I was riding alone,
staying alive, avoiding trouble,
including the backs of trucks,
by slowing down in lots of time.
It didn't matter that I had Ls,
because in those days, long ago,
Ls were able to be renewed, again and again.
Until they weren't.

Until I was relegated to pillion,
and until I gave it up, because of the pillion
who rode a while inside me.

Yes, I wasn't a good rider, quick and assured.
No, I didn't die, so perhaps I wasn't so bad.
Just once, on the freeway, I almost made 100k.
Just once I dropped it, outside a café.

PS Cottier

Central Australia

Thorny devil in the road –
we swerved, me mere pillion
not seeing him until we stopped,
sweet Moloch near the motorbike.
His thorns no match for rubber tyres,
he doesn't know how close we came
to levelling them all. He moves off,
strange rocking gait, as if an old film
played backwards for a few frames.
We remount and leave him
to ants, more ants, and near misses,
where safe red is cut by deadly tar.

PS Cottier

National Trail Sestina

For Sue and Leigh

It was Kidman who envisaged it, along the route
of travelling stock. North to South, country
traversed along the eastern coastal range, a distance
of more than five thousand kilometres, light
years away from noise of super-highways. Just silence
apart from hooves and boots along our National Trail.

Packing only essentials, sturdy mountain bike to take the trail,
good lungs, strong thighs and calves, our route
winds through scrub and sand, gully, river, plain. Silence
of unmade roads, bush tracks, fire trails across the country.
Necessity requires we travel light
with dread, and nerves, hoping we make the distance

planned. One day's ride to water, a distance
that seems easy, mapped, along an inked in trail.
Pedal out, fresh at first light
until the reality of the ride, toughness of the route
tests, subdues. It's up to us to meld and blend with country,
to do the miles, make a camp, in evening silence.

Birds already roosted, watering hole or creek meander, silence
until the frogs, night sounds of owl, howling dingo. Distance
seems different in unwalled dark. Country
is ever present, night overwhelms, opens to the spirit of the trail
leading us along an ancient route
where First Nations people walked and slept in starlight.

Before breaking dawn, pack saddlebags by firelight.
Heat our breakfast coffee, voiceless, just silence
and gathering our resolve and strength for whatever the route
today will throw at us. Just make the distance!
Find the markers, breathe in the trail.
Tread softly, gentle wheels, leave no damage to the country.

For unmarked time Custodians hold sacred this country
with its hidden water, secret places, blazing sunlight
marking like veins of blood the track and trail.
Frontier wars barricade their knowledge against invaders. Silence
until, with metronomic push on pedals, we come to learn. Distance
scarcely seems to lessen. Stage by stage we ride the route.

Mindfulness of trail, dusty grit of country.
Waterholes along the route, lie still, hidden in light
of sun and stars. In silence we survey the distance.

Sandra Renew

clogged concrete (haiku)

clogged concrete
two-wheeled surgeons
arteries open

PS Cottier

late evening

late evening
when I arrive home
your bicycle
leans askew
on the veranda post

Sandra Renew

Climate change (no gears)

So you spend *only*
a few hundred on the ancient bike
and a couple more for couriers
to bring it by road
from Victoria
in a big fart of
a delivery truck.

So you *had* to buy
a purple and orange
crocheted seat cover
from the United States,
which winged its way
to distant Canberra
like an ironic parrot.

And that basket!
Espied on Etsy,
woven in Thailand
(where the right reeds grow)
flown South, again,
but only seven or eight
thousand kilometres
this time.
Hardly a distance at all.

And now you ride it,
thirty minutes
every other day,
along the bike paths,
a proud little cyclist,
consumed by excellence.

Recycling a bike is good.
Cycling is good for the air.
You have done your bit.
Now breathe the breath
of safe-seated virtue.

Listen for the jangle of fallen tools.

PS Cottier

Cylinder 4

Always the issues

Puffing

The ballooning starts at seven.
Chest expands. Stomach retracts.
Mirror placated, it puffs out, relaxed,
as he hits the speeding road.
His skin has a mottled, murky hue,
somewhere between purple and red.
Tapir's snout wobbling over a fag,
he puffs his way to work, honking.
At the office, importance inflates him.
He frightens secretaries for a job.
Sometimes he gets excited.
(There are frogs in the desert
who puff themselves up
at the first hint of moisture.)
Fortunately, the girls run faster,
quick fleeing featherweights.
On the way home, he felt his heart
flutter. It's nothing, he thought,
just a bloody murmur,
a lunch burp unburped.
But in a puff of smoke,
the V8 left the road.
From under the wreckage crawled
a purple spotty toad.
(The largish dragon, seen nearby,
was never properly identified.)

PS Cottier

The last time

A half-heard noise, constant static,
the radio reports who did what
to who, and how that last sad who
is the one to be shamed.
She pulls out of the drive.

Each time she's had to move
to find a place safer, if not safe,
always, in the pea-green Honda,
she carries, tucked behind her seat,
two pot-plants to place in pride of place
in the new place. Hopefully
a house where they can stay
for longer this time,
long enough for the lily
to open some white flowers, stamens
glowing yellow as a comfort of candles,
and for the palm to have a parlour,
or at least a shelf to call its own.

She packed their things, and they move on,
one more time, the Jazz seeking harbour
up the highway. Two tired kids,
two plants just hanging on,
and her keyed determination,
refusing a future swollen, bruised,
or encircled in a boundary of hate.
There's the constant possibility
of a garden in some town, just a turn,
a turn or two more, and a few hundred
kilometres of needful flight.

The line on the road is a thin white ribbon.
She aims the car at somewhere new.

PS Cottier

The revenge of the dead woman plot starters

The bridge arches into the sky, an unlikely curve, a span too far.

In a mosquito singing swamp, under a floodplain bridge, by the side of a cane field road, in a run-down apartment somewhere unremarkable, an up-market luxurious sea view penthouse, an isolated stairwell, a parked Holden Torana, a dumpster in a Coles carpark, a seedy path in the darkness under a Moreton Bay fig…the body of a young, 'attractive' woman, death, blood, rucked up clothes…

Human interest guaranteed by a helpless, unfortunate, female body as victim. Now the plot is started. Mystery, Intrigue. Salacious forensics detail the violence, hatred, misogyny.

Now here is the photo board of the plot starters, a veritable smorgasbord of murdered femininities. But, and here you need to stay with the plot, they are moving, nodding, chatting with the portraits to either side, above, below, their high-level social skills (expected of the feminine) in play as they get to know each other. 'What is your story?' they ask each other. 'How did you come to be here? What foul play is the game you were forced into?' They turn like milk. Recalibrate the plot. Make lists of plot starters that are independent of the dead feminine.

Their targets, the authors of the plots that lack imaginative prowess to find something original. The readers of the plots who demand a recognisable reason for the heroic protagonist(s) to bend their skills and prowess to finding a solution, which however wrought will not bring the dead victim back to life. Advertisers and publishers who profit with more than reputation. And the social discourse which has for centuries cast the feminine as victim, preferably dead so she cannot talk back.

From the lists of plot starters there is one stand-out, the dismembered car. The strategy – replace the death of the feminine with an available car, wrong time, wrong place scenario, the perennially sexy 1961 EK Holden, burgundy duco, cream on top. Suitably ducoed, chromed, sweetly curved, finned, blacked tyres, mag wheels, connectivity, tinted windows, black bumpers. But dead.

Hence the overpass, the outsize span, the options for placing a mutilated body, parts pillaged, doors askew, back section with boot entirely removed by blow torch to become a trophy seat talking point in a trendy café in a trendy historic country town. In any case, the plot starts with the dead car, body parts missing, rusted, abandoned, sprung seats, stray dog palace, chicken coop, cracked, sunburst windscreen, wipers askew. Scratched, vandalised, wrecked. Written into the plot starter of every crime, mystery thriller novel or script. Twists and turns of plot, story and thrilling conundrum on page one, perpetrators and dastards tracked, trapped, tripped up. Freeing the feminised victim to play the hero, Sherlock Holmes or Hercule Poirot, Clint Eastwood or John Wayne, tough as nails, seen-it-all crime-stoppers.

Sandra Renew

This boot is a fridge

A response to 'The revenge of the dead woman plot starters' by
Sandra Renew

The salesman notes the waiting family, husband, the gorgeous
wife and girl-child with golden hair, and also clocks the
presence of the Murderer, who we shall call M, lurking
around the salesroom, hiding behind the hatchbacks.
Salesman turns to Husband. This new model Lantern has a
huge boot, he explains, suitable for carrying the feminine
driver of the narrative, who is not your actual driver, but
more the scenery upon which you will play out your
elaborate detective efforts, despite the police saying *Leave it to
us. It's too dangerous.* She may be cut into small pieces, lots of
them, and your gorgeous daughter too, which is why the size
of the boot is important. This boot is as big as a fridge. Bigger
even. May I suggest that you do not stump up for the
makeup mirror in the front passenger seat? She won't be
needing that! Salesman laughs, and M chuckles. Husband
looks vaguely concerned, as if he's lost something somewhere
but he can't remember what or where. But he knows he is
about to star in the drama of his tracking M through streets
as mean as cliché, and someone needs to die, as the salesman
said. His she (or shes) is the necessary loss onto which he will
write his eight-episode heroism. He buys the Lantern, and an
extra carpet for the boot. That's thinking ahead, says the
salesman. M nods his approval. Wife and daughter say
nothing, or nothing that that the narrator will recall.

PS Cottier

all part of the backstory

barmaids and get-away cars
Holden vans and see-through blouses
the first, nondescript, disappearing into street-scapes
the other, thrusting nipples into leering faces
watchers-on we see movement towards unbelief
or disbelief, all part of the backstory
like Cassandra's warnings, not believed

the barmaid ad's a shocker
willing to wear a see-thru blouse
willing to use your woman's body
to bring in the drinking swill crowd
of the undiluted masculine
not needed in the drive-through
because there they are in their cars
warm and cosy cocooned in metal and chrome
embraced by their other sex object

Sandra Renew

Wheels like the rings of a tree

My daughter sheds her P plates
I am old

She has her full licence
I am older

One day I will lose my licence
pillion in a hearse

No leathers necessary

PS Cottier

GP or not GP

You might have thought
that cars would even things up
between men and women;
size or natural speed
less important than horsepower.
After all, at the Olympics,
don't men and women
do the horsey things together?
But no, the famous drivers
are all men; it's Lewis,
not Louise. You might ask why?
I have no answer.
Reflex reactions mention reflexes.
Day to day, on the road,
it seems men may take more risks,
but the best drivers are controlled,
not reckless, not unrestrained.
They used to say women
could not be pilots,
and now they bomb, strafe and kill
with the rest of them.
They used to say a lot of things.
(And some still do.)
The famous drivers are all men;
is that a given or just a when?

PS Cottier

Car wash

From a car wash off the highway, where a B road meets a
country road, in a village overtaken by inexorable expansion,
it's so suburban. No valet is available, use self-serve hose and
sponge, and detergent by the bucket load. A car emerges into
sunshine, gleaming, polished, chrome fittings really dazzling.
And drives flamboyantly, with style and flair, towards a
promise of a future.

Left inside the car wash, all evidence of gender fluidity,
deliberate or accidental, however you want it construed, and
his/her/their masculine identity, like
washed-right-out-of-her-hair musical history. Now they're
clean and new and shiny, like a car that's been detailed with
no residual binary. It's amazing what a spruce up, spick and
span, gendered, identity-blurring androgyny can do.

They're clearly ambivalent and gender fluid, no brakes on
them, they're off the tracks of rigid presentation as either
woman or man. She/he/they are free of all that. It's amazing
what a discursive clean up can do.

Sandra Renew

Underground car parks

These are not dark, peaceful places,
in which water drips, somnolent,
forming limestone noses, snotty stalactites,
that cling to the roof for quiet centuries.
Sound here is amplified and muffled,
bringing murder to mind. A pillow is placed
over the normal face of day, and sunshine
rendered only a rumour. Always that orange
synthetic glare revealing sordid scum of
oil stains, and pillars sporting paint scrapes,
a forensic feast of car skin shed on giant fingers.
There is a barrier at entry, a possible guillotine
or at least, a stick to beat your car with,
for the sharp audacity of seeking entry.
A ticket spits out, and you stretch to take it.
Nosing into the always too small space,
minimised for the sacred demands of profit,
you do your best to respect the imperious
demands of white lines. Opening the door,
that smell of exhaust and piss, crushed chip,
hidden anxiety, and spilt coffee assaults you.
You check you have put on the handbrake
and locked the door several times,
then walk the walk of the recently damned,
dodging cars speeding toward the last space.
You shop, and pay the ticket, and return,
reverse, then thread the car through
narrow concrete tracks, to feed paper
into the car park troll's letter box.

Hard not to see the doom of civilisation
in these rectangular-marked hells,
these battery farms for four-wheeled hens.

PS Cottier

Cylinder 5

Apart from cars

9 a.m.

is wrapped in commuter cold
hunkering into bus seats
or nursing cars through bowels
of constipated traffic.
9 a.m. is the cruellest hour.
See the people made beige
pushing through scarfed
awakening, the workday's
reckoning, swapping
presence for credit.
The swaddled brutality
of 9 a.m., the coffee clutched,
the earbuds distracting
with a different rhythm.
Stomachs grumble cereal,
phones bring news
of elsewhere, but here
and now is the relentless
decanting of the day
through the funnel of 9 a.m.
This is the vampire hour,
not dusk. The light husk
of possibility drifts,
quite drained, no later than
9.10.

PS Cottier

U-turn permitted

He's there, dressed in fluoro
workout gear, a little Olivia Newton-John,
a little *Flashdance*, and he's riding
a skateboard up and down the U.
Fast down the side, through the bottom lip
of lettered smile, and slowly climbing back up.
Sometimes he hangs for a moment
in the white painted sky of the sign,
breaking free of the constant rolling
valley of U; unconstrained by
the grudging kerning of authority,
doling out its one permission:
go back where you came from.
A small parrot hovering, he tries to work
into the middle of the space between
the two fingers of the U, to become,
for eternity, a sweet umlaut,
for at least the wheels of his board
will punctuate the slippery U.
One day he will become an accent,
plant himself just so, and wave.
There'll be no more Sisyphus,
no more up and down and back,
although he quite likes the motion,
rocking through the U cradle
again and again and again.

It is his lullaby and heartbeat,
his gentle, permissive rumble.
He is sometimes audible to unruly ears,
ears pressed to the sign at 3 a.m.,
that catch his rolling motion in their cups.
The noise is forgotten in the hangover,
the hangover worn like a U-turn,
as wine runs, surely, to its ugly end.

PS Cottier

Pretend you've got a skateboard

Pretend you've got a skateboard, his father says. *Like this.*
Down, up, turn, down, up, turn… I'll be just over here,
unloading the rubbish. Pretend you've got a skateboard…

Arms wide, he runs, too fast for safety, down the concrete
incline, stumpy baby legs struggling on the smooth cement of
the up. *I'm flying* he shouts, wings in the air. *I'm flying!!!*

Sandra Renew

Metronome tanka

metronome
marking time on bin day
Fridays like clockwork
garbage truck yearns
to be a recycle truck

Sandra Renew

Trawl

There's a line in the water
between the rough and the smooth
A wind path, ruffled, broken, dark
And oil smooth light, unmoving
Daring you to look
into and down
Ground chains, winches coupled with outriggers
Prawn trawlers, looking nowhere but net wise.

Sandra Renew

Gagarin's death

Yuri Gagarin, first human being in space, died on a training flight in a MiG jet on 27 March 1968

Some say it was the weather,
and others far too much fuel;
and of course, conspiracies
always have their murky place.

Personally, I believe it was
a simple swarm of birds.
Not envious, not teaching
a Soviet Icarus a thing or two.

I think they just came to see
a man who'd seen much more
than any stonechat who knows
Summer Siberia and Winter Japan.

At least you died in flight.
Some things just have to be.

PS Cottier

Night bus station

i departures

buses lined up like caterpillars digesting the garden,
waiting for metamorphosis into night-infatuated moths insatiable,
wanting more…
drivers eating again crumbs falling on shirt fronts
excessive tomato sauce to make a pie more palatable,
wanting more…
uniform shirts straining
over sedentary bellies
international students, outsize bags spilling open taking in more
coming and going
electronic manifest scrolling ticketless travel
children using the empty space for impromptu ballet
embracing the polished unclean floor
in screaming practice

ii waiting in arrivals

six-year-old swings feet flicks hair
and it falls like a shroud –
balances on the backs of the seats
arms outstretched, voice-shrieks high above the conversation and
rumble of wheelie bags – *look at me*
she can fall either into the glass window
or into the path of the moving buses

Sandra Renew

Night bus

i sandwiches in brown paper

there's the bus station for the night bus
there's waiting and reading the tiny screen and repacking
there's sandwiches in brown paper
there's warm soft drink in crushable, rip-top cans
there's eating, unwrapping, repacking
there's last minute instructions, boarding announcements
there's repacking, eating, luggage-wheeling
scrabbling through bags and suitcases and repacking
there's greeting and hugging and hand shaking
and queueing and repacking and eating
there's ticket buying, and ticket rereading, and ticket finding
and losing
and repacking on the run and finding the bus and checking
which window
and phoning and texting and scrolling
there's announcement listening and queueing and boarding
and waving goodbye

roast beef sandwich
yesterday's white bread and last week's mayo
mustard and tangy cheese
he's driving through the night
bus full of silent passengers

ii boarding

you're just a girl in red and black, hands closed over your face
waiting, leaning, outside the bus, beside the queue
inside, the driver's console is dark, unattended
the seats are filling up and you are not moving
the window behind you, past you, opens up the street outside
why do you wait in the space between?

our overnight bus reflects in the panel behind you
windscreen wiper arms held together like hands in prayer
or a judgemental parent waiting for explanation

iii hiding in our uniforms

look at us lining up for our photo in blue uniform shirts
we're a bit smug because we're good civic citizens
going to a conference dressed neat and clean
shiny in our haircuts and arm folded pride
we're not even noticing the anarchy around us –
behind us the buildings burn, men in smoked uniforms blast
in the windows
children starve and beg, widows are cast out and cast off
their bruises livid neon-lit warnings that the world is not right
our blameless hands are clasped behind us now,
our shirts still pressed and clean, pristine

Sandra Renew

Entraining

There are lines, already laid down,
but the train reads them into life
twice a day.
The train is the poet.

The girl, picking daisies,
pollen-dusted, awaits the longer chain
joining cities.
The train is the poem.

The lovers' kiss, glanced through window,
and we feel their rock, the sure
electric cradle.
The train is poetry.

Reading the lines –
joining the cities –
holding the land –
in its gentle rhythm
of traverse.

PS Cottier

Truck

Birdsville to Bedourie is a short stretch of bitumen when you measure it
against the total kilometres of highway available for coming out in this
empty country, but it's long enough.
Thanks for stopping, Driver – What's your name, anyway?
Aaah, Felicity –
you're known as Feral? That's good, that's interesting…
So, Feral, I saw you earlier, back at the truck-stop, you know, we both tried
for water from the taps in the Ladies (it has a picture of a woman in a ball
gown so I'm pretty sure you knew it was 'our' room). Yes, I know it could
have been much improved with a bit of a clean, but who is left to do it? I
quit the café job last Monday, on the off-chance. Can I ask you something?
Feral? In a monster truck like this, where do you sleep? Oh, you don't?
My tattoo is just wishful thinking at the moment, Feral, but I love what
you've done with the ink – on-coming headlights making movies of your
arms…so cool!

Those multicoloured wings, do they go right over your
shoulders and arms?
The double women's sign on the back of your neck, I get it,
the personal is
political! And those rainbow stars are just floating up your
neck into your
hairline, wow…
OK, of course I can do a smokable rollie – where's the Drum
and papers?
No, I'm not a smoker myself, but it's not a deal-breaker when
you get down
to it. Is it lonely here on the road, Feral? Is someone waiting
for you in the
Isa? Yes, I do talk a lot when I'm not sure what the hell I'm
doing. Yes, I
will shut up now.
You've done something with your hair since you were
through here on
Monday, number 4 clippers, I guess, really makes a
statement. What, stalking
you? No, that's a big word!
Feral, what's the nightlife like for a girl in the Isa?…
Of course, I'm up for it. I'm out here, aren't I…?

Sandra Renew

Bobby Dazzler and the tractor-pulling contest

they came by ute to woo her
Sugar Princess of the Festival
seductress of the Sugar Country Motor Inn
dazzled by her beauty, centrefold or pin-up
check her out, you bloody beauty
bloody oath and bloody ripper, she's a bottler
I didn't warm to our Sugar Princess
until I saw her tractor, a Massey Ferguson
modified from vintage true. They left by ute, deflated,
when they saw her high on mishaps, fails,
fires, wild rides and the carnage of the
utes and tractors, everyone was high on pulling-fuel
good onya mate, a toughened Princess
goddess, fair dinkum Venus for our modern day
hot as a true-blue bobby dazzler.

Sandra Renew

Cylinder 6

Utes

In the back of this poem

there's a dog,
not a kelpie, balancing,
but a fat Staffie, snuffling.
The poem goes fast around corners.
It picks up words and slings them
into the back (*move over fatty!*)
There's room in the front for two,
but it's better when the poem drives itself,
not Tesla-y, but with its own unseen hands.
It grips the wheel, at 10 and 2.
Red as any riding hood, red as pox,
this poem revs its V8, musically,
and sometimes even plays its horn.
A utility poem, it can do all sorts.
Climb in the tray (*move over fatty!*)
lie down snug, lest there be cops,
and it'll take you out, out for a spin,
far from any pastoral routes,
into the clustered streets
and through slim, light volumes of thought.

PS Cottier

Scorpio to Venus: Love song 1977

I always think of my Sandman Holden ute as a dyke vehicle.
I've perfected the finger-wave to acknowledge its country-boy
rellies you find ubiquitous on Route 83 out of the Isa or even
on the narrow bitumen of the Newell past Goondiwindi. But
that dyke ute did us all proud at the beaches and coastal
highways where dirt roads and off-road and four-wheel drive
was over-kill looking for roadkill.

The first owner of my ute was a male person, Scottish
descent, age 24, named Bruce. He was killed, and also his
mother (no name given) when they were on the unstable
road shoulder near Boulia taking a breather in the noise of
the night silence. They heard one road-train, didn't realise it
was two, passing on top of them, and stepped back too late.
But the ute was fine, not a scratch or a bruise and still as red
and gorgeous as it had ever been. The thrill of the V8 on
ignition, new radial tyres, radial tuned transmission. How
could I not think of her as one of us.

The Sandman was not your average ute. It's true, it was not
yet the Kingswood, but there was no sense of playing an
instrument with one string. That engine was the whole
four-piece rock band, right there, in the interplay of clutch,
accelerator and brake.

The thing you should know, much more than your own discomfort, and theoretically true, is that with a dyke holding the key, that ute could pull the chicks. That ute was a chick-magnet, bringing with it, its own cloud of dust. And with two girls up front, it focused the attention of the boys with their surfboards, faded board shorts, and broken boxes of *Mr Zogs Quick Humps Sex Wax* in the pockets of their windcheaters.

I kept that beauty of a ute as clean as Bruce's mother had left it, as spick and span as any house-proud dyke with her eye on a good thing. Where will my atoms go when I die? They'll mix and meld with the Sandman, ride that V8 rumble through Scorpio to Venus.

Sandra Renew

Note: *Mr Zogs Sex Wax* was introduced in 1972 and quickly became the first choice for professional surfers.

there's a shed load of pigs out there

my cousins took me pig hunting *There's a shed load of pigs out there, big ones,*
it's National Park land, illegal as hell I was eight they were twelve and eleven.
aunts and uncles were in the backyard dark, around the fire pit, not minding us...
as always, they had tinnies, family grudges, schadenfreude, vindications to hash out.
the cousins took their dad's truck, rolled it down the driveway, no noise and no lights,
rifles wrapped in hessian bags clamped in the back, a big bastard of a spotlight
three uncontrollable yellow-eyed pig dogs, berserk with anticipation, skidding around the back-tray slobber dog-stink filthy breath teeth.
mountain gullies, washouts, low scrub, high trees, rotting logs roaring, bucking, rearing, braking – grunt and squeal of running pigs – chasing boys, curses, yodelling dogs, gunshots!
in the truck I crouch on the floor, ear on the cadence of the engine, listening for warning coughs and splutters, pressing on the accelerator to keep the spotlight on.
cousins straggle back, already rehearsing the size of the pigs, how many, so close and nearly.
no blood on their skinning knives, no grunt and heave of a dead pig into the truck tray, no scent of death or dying, just the smell of discharged shot, boy bodies, sweat, desperate energy, thrilling, running, the chase stretching, falling, sidestepping, dodging, weaving

afterwards, there was a keeping to the dark edges of the house
to avoid a thrashing. boys and dogs and an eight-year-old girl
had been where they shouldn't.

I never saw a pig alive or dead, never saw the mountain or the
swamp, only the inside of the cabin and a cone of light
cutting into nothing

Sandra Renew

Near Goondiwindi

So we're on the bike, me pillion,
and we pull up to refuel,
and there's a ute, parked nearby,
with a dog in the back.
I decide I'll see if he's nice enough
to pat, and walk quietly towards
the battered white tray.
I'm about to cautiously advance a hand
when I realise that's no dog.
A huge boar, rope-bound, alive,
heading towards a probably grisly death,
in which dogs may well be involved, and gore.
And in that moment, vividly, comes the line
You're not in Canberra any more.

PS Cottier

One night in Melbourne, 1980s

Off to a see a band,
we climbed in the back
of someone's ute, lay flat,
so that no passing cop
would stop us. From under
a thin white blanket I smelt stars,
heard the comfort rattle of trams,
the conversations of pedestrians.
I could have sat up, reached out,
tapped them on the back,
a sudden ghost of fun.
He drove on, we hopped down.
Ask me today the name of the band,
and all you'll get is a blank look.
Who owned the ute? I couldn't say.
But until my end, I'll recall
the sweet metal womb of that ute,
and the giggling mewl in its tray.

PS Cottier

Mystery

They drove past, down at the coast,
then suddenly braked. I saw them, seven
traditional gnomes, more scowl than cute,
climb from the ute, all cap and boot,
pipe and spade, and walk into the bushes.
They formed a line, and began passing
something down, until the last,
who wore a green cap, not red,
flung it in the back with a thud.
A second thing followed, and I saw
a single wing poking out from rope.
The gnomes were passing fairies,
slinging them like sacks of wheat.
The vague flutter of wing showed
that the packaged fairies were alive.
Seven fairies for seven gnomes.
Then the gnomes climbed inside.
They accelerated off, quick,
past the BIG4 caravan park.
I shook my head. You don't see that
so very often, you have to admit;
a ute of unknown model and make.

PS Cottier

96

Not thought through

A response to 'Mystery' by PS Cottier

As the tabloids are reporting,
seven fairies have been bound in rope
and kidnapped from the forest by seven gnomes,
the nasty ones, with the dastardly intention
of transporting them by ute (unspecified)
down the highway and into fairy servitude.

The combined furious glare from seven pairs of fairy eyes
makes the youngest, smallest and least worldly
of the gnomes (green capped), travelling in the back of the ute,
unguarded against an all-out fairy mind-hunting attack,
nervously use his unbranded army knife to unfetter
the apoplectic fairies, releasing them to the wind buffet,
the ute (unspecified) speeding away, out from under them.

Oblivious, the six gnomes stuffed together
in the ute's twin cab, their unthought-through plan
unknowingly undone, chortle with the thought
of the upcoming fairy enslavement.

Everyone knows, except gnomes apparently,
that fairies believe gender is a fluid and contradictory thing,
shapeshifting being part of fairy magic,
and the gnomes would be better off,
better served so to speak, if they put some effort
into wooing some gnomish servants, wives or general helpmeets,
gnomes who would give gnomish consent to their enslavement,
and, in passing, gnomes who have worldly confidence to
purchase a ute of identifiable model and markings.

Sandra Renew

Cylinder 7

Consequences

Full

We used to drink
until we were drunk,
still standing but slurring,
stroked with alcohol's finger,
and get into the car and drive
through dim backstreets, slow,
with the presumed immunity of youth.
The car jumped like a wallaby
misplaced in the middle of Melbourne,
as we mistimed clutch and gear.
And, of course, reversing years,
I think what if a homeless person,
or another, stumbling drunk,
had wandered into the road?
Swerving with reflexes dumbed,
dumbed down to the level of slug
is not so easy. Yet
all we thought of was
avoiding the blue flash of police,
not potential pedestrians
reduced to sloppy humps
under drunken wheels.
Only because luck rode with us
strapped into the backseat,
whispering sweet spells,
did this not happen.

Now I won't even have one wine,
weighed down with the awesome
common-sense anchor of middle age.
There are road cops inside my head,
sampling my blood at night,
mental vampires of propriety.

PS Cottier

The amazing sinking car

We're in the underpass, at the top of the bank out of the wind,
leaning back on cool cement. Watching the deep swirl of
current around the pylons, twelve-year-old fingers pinching
the butts of hand-rolled durries. Silent, comfortable.

A Holden Torana, baby-shit brown, blue trim, ugly as, comes
down the embankment beside us, doors and boot swinging
open, headlights on, so fast it leaves the ground on the cliff
edge, launches out over the water. Angles head down, dives for
the bottom. Teddy bear in the rear window swings and waves.

Air bubbles stream to the surface, some sounding like rushing
wind, others hesitant, emerging in slow gulps and glottal
burps. Headlights burn, then dim and disappear as the last
glimpse of chrome bumper vanishes.

We sit, frozen in the moment, not reacting, cigarettes
burning down to our skin, eyes on the river and the amazing,
flying, vanishing car.

Then, above us on the road, a scuffle of boots on gravel,
voices coming loud then soft in the wind:
Mate, do ya think anyone saw us?
Yeah, no, no yeah. Don't think so.
Mate, do ya think the water will wash off our fingerprints?
Yeah, no, no, yeah. Mate. Dunno.

Sandra Renew

Toad Princes

we were out that night in the Holden ute
road through the cane fields slippery as all get out
downpour roaring and closing down the viewing distance
to a few feet
steam struggling to rise off the tarmac against the force of rain
the toad count rose, all those potential princes, under the wheels,
high beam picking them out, stunned but sanguine,
on both sides of the white line
while she gunned the engine, veered and swerved and yahooed
every time we got one,
squashed flat, bloody for a moment but then guts
sluiced away as storm water –
hanging out the windows to make the body count
sodden, dripping, high on adrenalin and the 'us' of it
empty half-bottle of Bundy flat on the floor in the footwell

Sandra Renew

Frogs at Durras

We bought the house, feeble fibro shack
walls thin as a yacht's, teetering near the sea.
The second time we drove there, slowly,
tentatively, nosing towards ownership,
rough jagged rain sawed through twilight.
We wondered if the house could survive.

Turning the corner, our eyes jumped,
jerked at a million tiny frogs revelling in rain,
the black streaming street a foaming river.
Each raindrop a watery egg, containing
tadpole, exploding into perfect frog
as it hit the tarmac, transmogrified.

I ran ahead of inching car, scooping throbbing fistfuls,
placing them on nature strip, dividing green from black.
And still they splashed and clung to sodden tar,
each splayed finger reading braille on the rough road;
indecipherable invitation to party, or to climb, perversely,
the dark warm curves of the crushing car.

Three years later, we sit in heat, and await the frogs
never seen since the Walpurgis abandon, that abundant night.
Sometimes we have heard them, piping, tinkling, muted bells,
signalling to each other, chirruping reminders
as they wait beneath rocks, huddled in just damp dark
that the drought must break. Our house still stands.

PS Cottier

What do you call it when your heart is broken

I hope she was worth it scrawled in luminous, yellow paint,
defacing the shine, from headlights to back wheel guard. Both
sides of the deep maroon custom-painted duco, once
gorgeous, dripped and splashed on the chrome accenture.
Gouged into the bonnet with some sharp metal
revenge-maker, an uncontrolled *F-you* and the date. And final
indignity, windows smashed into dazzling webs. Imagine
driving through the streets in full view, downtown to the body
shop. More than a tag, this is revenge-hatred art, a give and
take, a lose-lose, the only victim is the Mercedes-Benz W108.

Sandra Renew

Take one small vase of roadside flowers

take one small vase of roadside flowers
pick it up from the floor out of the way of crushing boots
replace it on the packing crate table
let it sit in the silence of the empty shipping container
let the small plastic truck, stable enough on three wheels, sit
beside the vase
let the concussive boom of big guns, rattle of AK 47s,
the grenades, the IEDs
come closer, vibrate the metal walls,
expend itself on nothing –
let the empty room wait

Sandra Renew

Two views

1. Momentary

The phone-check in the car,
that glance down, and up,
one hand held at breast height.
It means nothing, nothing at all,
until a motorbike is rear-ended,
because Twitter was going off
and nervous eyes could not wait.
Denimed legs twist to pretzels,
and skin hangs like washing,
pinned to a zigzag line of bones.
Then the phone will be sifted
for informational nuggets,
police the avid gold-diggers.
The one more glass of wine,
sipped, innocuous until it isn't,
and a child paints the crossing
with red stripes as well as white,
her head the clotted brush.
These everyday rebellions,
ninety-nine percent safe,
even ninety-nine point nine.
Tiny as viruses, these everyday
misdemeanours surround us,
a quiet cocoon of rebellion.
Until the sting of accident,
the unfolding wasp wings
of what we will call luck
or fate land on our wheel,
and unfold into certainty.

2. Lapse

One second, more or less,
I pray I might replay
that morning,
rewrite the way I woke her.
Either forced haste upon her,
rushed the rituals
of hair, of clothes, of teeth,
or lingered, found her sick,
too sick to walk to school.

If fever, a sandpaper throat, a rash
of small stop signs had erupted,
we might have stayed,
eaten sweets
watched animals
swarm on TV plains.
But no kind illness intervened,
she dressed, brushed hair, we left.

Seven years, she had, seven years,
and she would show how much she knew.
Looking over shoulder,
she called my name
and turned back, and ran across,
and erased her dear short story.
She met the car, which could not stop.
Momentary pause, and screams.
My life on hold forever.

Hers has gone, her sweet seven
never floats up to eight,
soul's bubble smeared
on rude red road.
The moment tolls forever,
my hand grasps, too late,
for hers, in air, in empty heavy air.
Love remains, and that day,
looping through my mind.

PS Cottier

Jeep

You can drive it up a wall says the salesman at Dominion
Motors in Brisbane,
breathless with adrenalin and testosterone. *You can drive it
under water.*
In 1976 we had one of those Willys MBs, dirty green with
white military
numbers painted on the bonnet, Hurricane F-head,
four-cylinder engine
with overhead inlet valves and side exhaust. Axe and shovel
mounted on
the side, open top, flat canvas driver's seat, left-hand drive.

The live axle on leaf springs made it ideal for the washed-out
tarmac roads
and sand-scoured bush tracks trying to get through the
mangroves to the
beach and reef, where floods and cyclones and monsoons
riled up the
crocodiles and extended invitations to the cane toads. We
often took our
jeep out to the coast so we could cool down in the tepid,
slow-moving sea,
and then ended up digging, winching, pushing, covered in
sand and mud,
cursing inelegantly for overextending the little vehicle's
capabilities.

But, that morning we were on the Bruce Highway, out of Townsville,

heading north. In the front passenger seat, my girlfriend was stripped to

her knickers, sunbaking through the windscreen and the open top. She

had thrown her clothes, shirt, trousers, bra and socks, piece by piece, into

the back footwell behind her seat, then, as they rose and filled with air,

threatening to fly out behind us, she tossed her heavy, non-tropical Doc

Martens over her shoulder on to the floor to weigh them down.

Bare feet up on the dash locker handle, she had ABBA and Stevie Nicks

down on air guitar, then air keyboard, crescendo, riffs and licks, knowing

she could be famous; head banging, seat dancing, singing any of the words

she could remember, making up new ones in the gaps…

Two things happened.

A muscular tarantula ran up from the disturbed safety of the back footwell,

where it had been cowering under her pile of clothes, across her leg and on

up the inside of the front windshield. There it gripped with its toes and right

on the top edge, leaned into the wind. My reaction was immediate and not

pretty, using clutch and brake and accelerator all at once. The brake marks

we left on the hot bitumen later became legend, with random people from

the bar driving out from town to take photos with their Kodaks. But this

came later.

A police car pulled out behind us from an overgrown cutting on a side road,

lights flashing and came up dangerously close to our backend. The officer

gestured unmistakably that we should pull over. My first instinct, indicated by prior experience of the police, was to avoid stopping until my passenger found her clothes and got dressed in the front seat, but, given the spider situation, I was already onto the loose edge of the road shoulder and skidding to a stop.

At this point, my girlfriend was frozen in horror at the spider, the rock and

roll as we swung at speed off the bitumen into soft gravel, and the ominous

appearance of the police officer, who was by then out of his car, settling his

broad-brimmed hat onto his head and walking purposefully towards us. He was tall, six foot six, or more, and, as he loomed over the open top of the low-slung jeep, he cast a black shadow of doom over our excursion.

Ladies. How ya goin'? Can I help yous? said the police officer, leaning across

my girlfriend's naked body, flicking the spider off the windscreen as an

afterthought. He only has eyes for the instrument panel, the wire-thin

steering wheel, fold-down front windscreen, insect eyes side mirrors. *What*
model is this? M38 or CJ-38?

Sandra Renew

White lines

In Western Australia once I almost forced a police car from
the road, swerving back in after overtaking, to avoid inching
over double white lines. They pulled me over, and I said
Sorry, officer, I'm not used to these conditions. They let me go,
and I drove on, unscathed and laughing. Only later did I
think how lucky I was, and then again, that maybe it wasn't
just luck that allowed me to drive away. Who might not be
allowed a free pass regarding those clear white lines?

PS Cottier

Courtesy

'That one can show a great deal of courtesy to other cars and to general traffic is assured, but that few people do is also a fact.'
– Dorothy Levitt, *The Woman and the Car: A Chatty Little Handbook for all Women Who Motor or Who Want to Motor* (London: John Lane, 1909)

Cute wave of acknowledgement to another car of the same make
Over the crossing we walk, pretending to run, swinging arms
Unlikely as it seems, the four-wheel drive let me in, and I
wave again
Riding my bike I slow down before overtaking the old
woman and her ratty dog
Tailing the rusty Toyota, I back off, leaving space for its rumblings
Even the cockatoos demand that I give them space as I pass
the nature strip
Silly guy crosses the road on his phone, against lights, and I
don't toot
You are driving like a dickhead. I just turn up the music. I hum.

PS Cottier

Seasonal nomads

Restless souls, itinerant drifters, our forward momentum
minuscule, we smell the rain, newly fallen on dry earth and
parched eucalyptus, before the earth is slaked, seasoning of
petrichor rising around us, looking ahead, asking *what is free?*
Thinkers of the universe, banging our pots and pans, tapping
at the edges, mending where we can.

seasonal nomads
caravan trailing an unreliable rig
track the backroads
fruit harvest, digging potatoes, working a yabby farm
retirement shelved for a living wage

Sandra Renew

Cylinder 8

Further on

Capitalist converters

'Canberra thieves target catalytic converters for rare metal'
– *The Canberra Times*, 25.07.21

Platinum, palladium and rhodium –
thieves squash themselves under cars
flatter than thirsty lizards of cliché
and convert catalytic converters into cash.
And the real crime is how
these metals are mined in the first place,
by people dwelling in poverty relentless as iron
before ores are refined and wedged under cars
all errant blood washed off, shiny as dreams,
so our precious air stays nice and clean.
Metals reach the buyer's side of the market –
no slave labour here in Canberra!
Just the occasional, minor crime
and muffled screams from beneath.

PS Cottier

My application for Space Fleet was refused

The splashed Pollock-paint of the stars, even the relatively
mundane sight of Earth through the porthole (a swollen
puffer-fish in an aquarium) are not for the eyes of those with
questionable mental resources, they said in the reply. Yet
perhaps those used to solitude could easily negotiate the dull
heaviness of the spaces between familiar here and
indecipherable *there*. Year after grey-toned year, I have carried
my own gravity. I have known the anchored weight of getting
by. Crawling between the planets, those long yawns of
waiting, might call for one used to her own consolations, her
own thought-out constellations, rather than the social maps
of those who shine like stars.

PS Cottier

On the death of the V8

That deep rumble, gut churning glee,
planting pure delight on tarmac
will be lost in a lighter future –
the V8 a dinosaur that farted excess
into the world's thin ring of air.
Rightly so, we say, for who needs
such a monster of pungent power?
And yet, is it wrong to grieve
for all the utes, all the Commodores
and Falcons, shined to mirror
that delicate sky, soon to zoom only
through thin streets of memory?
The skilled hands that assembled
the beasts, put the cylinders
where the cylinders needed to be,
also fading out of industrious now,
rendered redundant as corsets
or calling cards, erased from work
that made something glorious and alive,
and deadly as a steel-toothed shark.

I am no metalhead Miss Havisham,
clutching a chamois, all wept out.
And yet, when I die, I hope the chariot,
swinging down, is a lowered, purple V8.
Maybe the fetching angels
will do a few screeching blockies –
take the long the way up to the clouds
where St Peter waves a chequered flag.
(The devil drives a 4-wheel drive.)

PS Cottier

Ecosystem

Mustang orange
sweet taste of speed
tangy traffic

tangy traffic
I drop old peel
seedy carpet

seedy carpet
sprouts bright flowers
Mustang orange

PS Cottier

Engineering luck

First the model in clay,
honed to perfection.
This one will fly
through life; V8 avoiding
any potholes. The vehicle
is assembled, given to
some fortunate sod,
driving unconcerned.

That one is a pogo stick,
upon which the recipient
attempts to jump –
wobbling and wary.
See him fall off.
Watch him trying
to avoid insouciant cars
steered by the 'naturally gifted'.

PS Cottier

What is it called when you love your car?: On admitting to a mild case

admitting fascination for the mystique imbued in cars,
for some, a special car can stand in as avatar
but when you turn on the ignition
for your captivation there's immediate recognition
and deliberate opprobrium designed to upset and jar...

and there's slagging off or teasing your passion can mar,
in-group exclusion and derision that goes too far
causing painful social inhibition
for admitting fascination

so when a car is found that snags your heart, a star
of universe and galaxy, outshining everything close and far
away, just go with your intuition
bring ambition to fruition
stand your ground, hold up the highest bar
for admitting fascination

Sandra Renew

Note: Mechanophilia is a paraphilia involving a sexual attraction to machines such as bicycles, motor vehicles, helicopters, ships and aeroplanes. Mechanophilia is treated as a crime in some nations with perpetrators being placed on a sex offenders' register after prosecution. Wikipedia

Rondeau for love

I know a car as lover not as death
such beauty in design, I catch my breath
transport me in ecstasy, engineer my delight
precision perfection, a heart-catching sight
but a wealth drug more common than crystal meth

custom painted for love, a hair's-breadth
away from obsession, until 'the hundredth
car as weapon', headlines sensationally write –
I know a car as lover

war and blood overwhelms us, knowing the breadth
of cars co-opted in the cause of death
car bombs, drive-through protesters, date-rape sites
driving while drugged, high as kites
love always seasoned with reasons, not blind or deaf –
I know a car as lover

Sandra Renew

Bits

Car parts reveal themselves,
emerging from the ground;
coiled DNA bulbs of springs,
long lost mirrors blinking at the sun,
carburettors screwing up through dirt.

A gum tree sports an ancient car door,
one of its branches threaded through
by an anarchist mechanic, or sculptor,
blending wood and deathless metal.

At Lake Illawarra
a cormorant suns itself
on a tiny rubber island
of convenient tyre.

The bits last longer
than the bones
of the drivers.
Only the teeth
that once smiled
at the glorious speed
of all the parts combined
may last as long as this screw,
or this ridged sun of diff.

PS Cottier

Acknowledgements

The authors extend thanks to the first publishers of some of their poems in this collection.

Sandra Renew

'When did she become so lonely?', 'Weekend Canberra', 'Bikes', 'late evening', 'Night bus station', 'Night bus' and 'Take one small vase of roadside flowers', *The Orlando Files*, Ginninderra Press, 2018
'Suburban tanka', *The Canberra Times*, 10 July 2021
'walking both away and into', and 'Seasonal nomads', *Live Encounters,* 6 June 2021
'In the Hindu Kush' and 'Silent combat', *Who Sleeps at Night,* Ginninderra Press, 2017
'Truck', 'Bobby Dazzler' and 'Jeep', *It's the sugar, Sugar,* Recent Work Press, 2021
'Scorpio to Venus: Love song 1977', *Acting Like a Girl,* Recent Work Press, 2019
'There's a shed load of pigs out there' in *Mountain Secrets* anthology, ed. Joan Fenney, Ginninderra Press, 2019
'Toad Princes', *Other Terrain*, Issue 6, Swinburne University, 2018
'National Trail Sestina', *Tracks: Newsletter of the National Trail*, March 2022
'The Amazing Sinking Car', *Travel: An Anthology of Microlit*, ed. Cassandra Atherton, Spineless Wonders, 2022

PS Cottier

'Summernats (and Floriade)', *The Canberra Times,* December 2008
'Climate change (no gears)', *The Mozzie*, Volume 25 Issue 7, October 2017, republished *Utterly*, Ginninderra Press, 2020

'Puffing', *The Glass Violin*, Ginninderra Press, 2008
'9 a.m.', *Project 366*, June 2016 <http://project365plus.
blogspot.com>
'Gagarin's death', *The Mozzie*, Vol. 18 Issue 8, October 2010
'Entraining', *Poetry in Motion: A collection of poetry written
while travelling from Canberra to Sydney on the Poets Train 3
September 2012*
'U-turn permitted', *Quick Bright Things: Poems of Fantasy and
Myth*, Picaro Press 2016
'In the back of this poem', *Eureka Street*, Vol. 31 No. 8, April
2021
'On the death of the V8', *Utterly,* Ginninderra Press, 2020
'Engineering luck', *The Mozzie*, Vol. 28, Issue 10, May 2021
'the wrecked cars (haiku)', *AntipodeanSF*, Issue 279,
December 2021

Some poems first appeared on pscottier.com, the poet's blog.
Minor changes have been made to some poems since first
publication.

About the Authors

PS Cottier

PS Cottier lives in Canberra, drives a Mustang, collects gnomes, and writes poetry, which has appeared in a variety of publications in Australia and elsewhere. She has written six previous books of poetry, and edited *The Stars Like Sand: Australian Speculative Poetry* in 2014 with Tim Jones. She also writes non-fiction, book reviews, and short stories. PS Cottier is currently the poetry editor at *The Canberra Times*. She wrote a PhD on images of animals in the works of Charles Dickens at the ANU, and also completed a law degree at the University of Melbourne.

Sandra Renew

Sandra's poetry collections are *It's the sugar, Sugar,* Recent Work Press, 2021; *Acting Like a Girl*, Recent Work Press, 2019; and *The Orlando Files*, Ginninderra Press, 2018. *Acting Like a Girl* won the 2020 ACT Writing and Publishing Award for Poetry, and was shortlisted for the 2020 ACT Book of the Year. Sandra is a founding editor, with Moya Pacey, of the *Not Very Quiet* online journal of women's poetry and *Not Very Quiet: The anthology*, eds Moya Pacey and Sandra Renew, Recent Work Press, 2021.